The Girl Who Claims Anonymous: An Interview Down Memory Hell

ANDREA SAROZA

Cover design by Melissa Norris

You are my sunshine

My only sunshine

You make me happy

when skies are grey

You never know, dear

how much I love you

Please don't take

my sunshine away

Contents

INTRODUCTION

Our journey is going to be hard. It's not for the weak. Trying to heal from things you had no control over can be difficult. You may be battling with some demons that you are unaware of—and some of which you are fully aware. One of those demons you may be battling is something you may have caused yourself, and you may feel it's unforgivable. We will address those as well, so don't worry about that.

> *Warning:*
> To heal, we must acknowledge what happened in the past.

This book is my personal interview with She. Now, She nor I am a doctor or a counselor, and we don't have any degrees. She is just a person who has been through some things and was able to do something about it. *Let's address the elephant in the room first, shall we?*

She was hurting and in pain. She wasn't aware until she became an adult that everything she had been through was not normal. She was raised to be tough, push through situations, and move on. She ended up developing a cold-hearted persona. The truth was, she was crying out for help. Suffering and evil were building a foundation within her, that was indeed against God.

The first part of this book will cover all the challenges She has been through, recognizing and identifying aspects of her life that genuinely affected her. It is divided into "trauma categories."

She will share her memories and experiences per category in no order. The second part will provide the tools and techniques She used to get through it all.

Well, let's go down memory hell, shall we?

THE BEGINNING

Tell me about your mom.

I heard yelling in my kitchen. Although I couldn't decipher the conversation they were having, I knew it was intense. There was a lot of banging followed by screaming and crying. The distinct noise of furniture being moved around and different objects being dropped on the ground echoed throughout the house.

The curious child I was went to see what was happening. There they were, my mom and stepdad at the time, fist-fighting. Their backs were leaning against the white kitchen wall while he had her in a headlock, and she was punching him in the face. I started screaming and crying, yelling out, "Don't hurt Mommy!"

I was so scared. A set of keys was on the table, and I grabbed them and threw them aiming at his face. I wasn't thinking about what I was doing, it was just my instinct reaction to protect my mother. The keys flew right past him and slammed against the wall behind them without leaving a mark. I could hear my mom yelling, "Get the fuck off me! Don't do this in front of her!" I thought my mom was going to die. But the reality of it was... he was just trying to keep her under control and prevent her from continuing to hit him.

Suddenly, I was quickly grabbed and lifted off the ground by my older brother. He swiftly took me into our room and said, "It's okay. Mommy and dad are just fighting. It'll be over soon."

"But why is he hitting her?" I asked my brother, out of breath from my cries.

He ignored my question, and assured by saying, "It's okay, I got you." He put headphones over my ears and laid me in his bed. He was trying to protect and comfort me as a big brother should.

I fell asleep in his arms. Not too long after that, I was awakened by my mom hugging me and crying herself. She laid next to me as she was rubbing my hair in a comforting manner. Her face was marked by tears and was puffy and red—she'd obviously been crying for a while. She said, "I'm so sorry baby, I'm okay. I'm right here baby. I'm sorry you had to see that."

At that specific moment, as a young child—not even five years old—I knew I had to protect my mom at all costs.

Why did you feel you needed to protect her?

Overtime, my mom picked some crappy relationships to be in. She was a young mom and did her best with the situations that she was put in. She loved so hard but dated horrible men. She gave them her all, and in return, she got used and abused. I had seen my mom get into so many physical altercations by this point. Inside of me, I became her pit bull. I was not afraid to fight anyone or anything for my mom. She was working two jobs most of my life to provide for me and my sister. Although she had her flaws, she was a good mom and apologized when she was in the wrong. I also knew that she loved to smoke weed and drink to deal with her problems. It was bad enough that she was hardly around, but when she was, she was left to her demons. She was broken but did her best.

She tried to fill the void in her heart with the wrong things and the wrong people— *including Antonio.* Before I get into this story, I want to clarify that I used to refer to him as *"The Dominican."* I have nothing against Dominicans; I love all people. I chose to identify this man as such because growing up I hated him so much that I never called him by his name. This is why I refer to him as *"The Dominican."*

We lived in a small one-bedroom apartment. The thick dull colored walls of the apartment always made me feel uneasy and fearful. Often times when I was nervous as a child, I would stand in one section of the apartment and investigate every room in the house without moving my feet. It was my sister, my mom, him, and me living there. I was in the bedroom. One day, he and my mother started arguing in the kitchen. I was a preteen at that point. He started raising his voice, and when he did, I knew that it was time for me to intervene in the situation. I entered the hallway that led into the kitchen and yelled, "Hey! Lower your fucking voice when you're talking to my mother!"

He made direct eye contact with me. All I could see was rage. "Go back into the room! I got this! I'm fine!" my mom yelled back at me. Her face was red; I could tell that she was pissed off. She made a specific face when she was angry. Her eyes became focused on what she was looking at, like a shark staring at its prey. When she got really mad, and she would start tearing into people in aggravation.

I went back into my room but left the door cracked open so I could hear everything. I planted myself near the cracked door and I didn't move. I listened closely while they argued. Their volume began to increase, and I finally heard my mom scream out furiously, "Don't fucking spit at me!"

I heard the table and chairs begin to scrape against the floor of our small eat-in kitchen. When I heard what sounded like the table ferociously slamming against the wall, I swung open the bedroom door, ran into the kitchen and saw it happen... he slapped the life out of my mom and was pulling her hair.

Without a second thought, I quickly grabbed a butcher knife that was drying on our dish rack along with our other dishes and ran towards him screaming. He saw me coming and started running away from me as I swung the knife. I caught him with the point of it, but only enough to scratch the upper part of his back. He moved much more quickly than I did. I ran after him—out of our apartment, down the stairs, out the front door, and down the block—outrageously screaming at him.

My guy friends were playing football outside and saw me chasing this man with a knife, screaming and yelling that I was going to kill him. When I realized he was too fast, I turned around and ran back home to my mom. From the corner of my eye, I could see my friends were concerned. They watched me emotionally making my way back to my mother.

She was sitting on one of our kitchen chairs crying. I sat down next to her trying to catch my breath and make sense of what had just happened. I finally looked up and saw her suffering. I too began to cry.

"I'm sorry, baby," my mom said with tears in her eyes as her face began to swell. She held her head up high though. She was trying to make it seem like she was okay. I grabbed a rag, wet it with cold water under the kitchen faucet, and gave it to her. I grabbed ice and a rag for her. "If I ever see him again, I am going to kill him," I spoke.

I wish I could say she never saw him again, but she kept seeing him. She didn't bring him around me. It was a sad time for me. Not only was she still seeing the man who would hit her, but she spent less time with me because of it. I felt like she would rather be with him than be with me. She and I would often argue about this. She would say, "But I love him."

I noticed when she would have bruises. I would ask her what happened. Her response was always, "Nothing baby, I'm fine." She would fall into these depression spells. Often, she would cry, yet make it seem as if she were okay. My mom was always in pain.

My mom was just used to being abused. As I grew up, I got used to being her protector. Eventually, they broke up. But unfortunately, eventually my mom became the abuser. I ultimately ended up protecting a boyfriend of hers. She walked all over him, used him for his money, and beat the crap out of him.

He never laid his hands on her. He was the local drug dealer, but he was a good guy. He treated my mom like a princess, and she didn't care. He bought her whatever she wanted, helped her pay her bills, and was always there for her. It broke my heart to see what her boyfriend dealt with. She became an embarrassment.

Where was your father when all of this was happening?

My biological father didn't want anything to do with me. He made that clear to my mom when she was pregnant with me. Throughout my childhood, I saw him about ten times. I was missing a part of me that I had no idea about. *Rumor was that he engaged in the kind of life we won't mention...* but let's say a massive group of people were involved. I just wanted my dad.

How could you miss someone who wanted nothing to do with you?

As a kid I would ask myself, "Why didn't my dad love me? Where was he? Was he thinking about me? What did I do wrong that my dad didn't want me?" I missed him so much, but how could I miss someone I didn't know? I used to think would I still need to be a protector if my dad were around? Did he ever hit my mom? Would he have come to rescue me if he knew what I was going through? Would he rescue my mom from all her pain, too?

I wanted a protector so severely. To this point, every man

my mom was involved with showed me what I was asking for may only exist in the movies. I would cry myself to sleep, whispering, "Dad, if you love me, you'll come and find me."

Spoiler alert: He never showed up. I spent most of my life blaming myself and thinking I wasn't good enough. If it wasn't for my dad's parents, my grandparents, I don't think I would have ever met him.

The times I did meet my father it was like starting over every single time. I knew he was my dad, but he was a stranger. To me, he abandoned me. He left my mom to fend for herself. The times we spent together were awkward. Plus, he tried to talk crap about my mom, and it turned me off because no one was allowed to talk bad about my mom to me.

I was angry at him for not being there for me, but I was also angry at him because I felt like he didn't care to be in my life either. *It hurt.* He didn't want to be around, and I had to accept that. His actions showed me everything I needed to know.

Were any of your mom's boyfriends a father figure to you?

Yes, my stepdad who is my sister's father. When he and my mom broke up, he would pick me and my sister up every weekend. Well, it wasn't as often for me because, luckily, I spent most weekends and summers with my amazing grandparents (my dad's parents).

He was the only dad I knew. I wasn't treated equally though, that was for sure. After spending time with him, my sister always came back with brand new clothes and sneakers. He was a good dad to her. I was just happy he was still in my life.

One Friday, I decided to go to his house for the weekend. I felt the little girl in me get broken again that day. My sister and I ran outside after we heard my mom say, "Your dad is here!" We raced outside and greeted him with hugs and kisses.

My stepdad held my hand and took me to the side… I knew sad news was coming. He said in the softest, gentlest giant voice, "Baby, I want to talk to you really quick." I could hear the crack in his knee as he knelt eye level with me.

"You know I love you, right," he said while caressing my hands.

"Yes, dad," I replied.

"Baby, I'm so sorry I have to do this to you, but I can't take you with me anymore," he said with watery eyes.

"Why did I do something wrong?" I said while looking down at my feet, trying to process what he had just said.

"Oh, baby, I was afraid you would ask me that. The truth is that you're not my biological daughter, and some people think I shouldn't have you with me anymore."

My heart sank. I could feel a knot in my throat start to form as I held back my tears. Afterward, he said, "I'm so sorry, baby. I will always love you."

With a clenched jaw, I replied, "It's okay." He hugged me, and once he let go, I turned away as if it didn't bother me. I went inside, zoomed up the stairs of our apartment building, and went straight to my room. My heart broke a little that day. Not only did my biological father not want me, but now my stepdad didn't either. I felt so unlovable. I felt like the only dad I knew didn't want me anymore. No more big soft hugs... no more fried eggs for breakfast... no more play fighting like the karate movies.

My mom loved eating friend eggs for breakfast and often times he would make them for her. He would coat the pan with oil. When it got hot, he would crack the egg in the pan. As the oil would begin to pop, he would whisper to himself, "Ow, shit! Dang it!" as it caught his arm hair. He would be scared to get burned but made the best fried eggs ever. I would tell him, "Dad it's okay you can make me scrambled eggs." I felt bad he would burn himself. But he was always on a mission to finish those eggs for us.

When we would karate fight, he would make the sounds with his mouth like in the movies. The famous Bruce Lee sound with the punching and kicking sounds. He was so good at it. There were times I couldn't even play fight because I was laughing so hard!

My dad was gone—the only one I knew—and once again, I was left feeling broken. My heart got ripped out of my chest. I loved him so much. As a child, I started to grow envious of my sister. She had a mom and a dad who loved her. We had two different lives under the same roof. There I was, the incomplete one.

After your mom and dad split up what happened next?

At one point, things got bad for my mom. My grandparents were trying to take custody of me because my mom was struggling to keep it together. It turns out that my mom backed out last minute. My mom tried her best, but I knew the truth at the end of the day. She was a product of an abusive mother and an abusive family where the men didn't know how to keep their hands to themselves.

My mom, *my poor mom*, was abused. Her sisters as well. Many of the women in my family were sexually abused. She was just a product of her environment. The women on my mom's side of the family suffered in silence. It was a demonic generational curse. They got abused by the men who were supposed to love and protect them. But according to my mother's mom, *"everyone gets touched."*

You mentioned your mom was struggling, did that affect you outside of your home life?

Yes. When I was in elementary school, I remember that I couldn't stand bullies. We didn't have much. Sometimes I went to school wearing shoes without socks because I either didn't have any or my mom couldn't afford to wash clothes at the laundromat.

I was sitting in class, and my teacher noticed a student wearing two different-colored socks. "Carlos why are you wearing one pink sock and one purple sock?" she said while laughing. The class also started to laugh at Carlos. I didn't. I put my head down. I didn't find it funny at all. All I kept thinking was at least he had socks while unintentionally shrugging my shoulders.

The teacher must have thought I laughed because she called out my name and said, "You shouldn't be laughing; at least he can afford socks."

I wanted to crawl up in a ball. I was filled with embarrassment. "I didn't even laugh at him!" I yelled back at the teacher.

"Yeah, sure." She replied in a sarcastic tone. She scoffed as she sat down on her chair behind her desk.

I got this sudden urge inside of me. I felt my face get hot and an overwhelming feeling of embarrassment took over me. Filled with pure anger, I grabbed my textbook, walked up to my teacher, and slammed the textbook into her face. She flew back, her feet went up in the air, and she landed right on the floor with her chair under her. I tossed my book aside and walked my angry little butt to the principal's office.

Walking through the hallway felt like an eternity. I was crying in the hallway as I was walking to the principal's office. My teacher followed behind with a vast bloody nose. I'm not going to lie; I felt like a bad ass. I couldn't believe what I just did, and I was shocked by my own actions. *It did feel good though to stand up for myself.*

My mom was not happy about this. The following day, my mom was in the principal's office listening to the story about the incident. My mom said, "I have a good kid. She wouldn't just do this out of nowhere," she then turned to me and asked the big question, "Baby, what did she say? What happened?"

I remember struggling to tell my mom what triggered this as I fidgeted with my fingers nervously. I finally built up the courage and said in a soft tone hoping only my mom would hear, "She made fun of me and said I couldn't afford socks in front of the whole class."

What happened next felt as if it was in slow motion. My mom stood up and walked straight into the hallway. In the hallway, she started yelling, calling out for my teacher. My teacher was standing in the hallway greeting her students as they entered the classroom for the morning. My teacher turned around and saw my mom speed walking towards her. My mother punched her right in the face. The security guard arrived just in time and separated my mom from her.

After the police showed up and calmed down the situation, we walked home. Once we got a few blocks away from the school, we got to a corner where the cars had the green light. We stood there waiting for our opportunity to cross the street. My mom faced me and started scolding me. "Don't you ever let anyone treat you badly. We may not have much, but we don't deserve to be treated like that. You always fight for yourself. Don't let anyone, *ever*, walk all over you baby. Anybody steps out of line with you, you fuck them up and don't stop until you see blood!" she yelled.

The young, frightened version of me said, "Yes Mom," as my voice cracked. I saw the pain in my mom's eyes. She was embarrassed, and I could tell she was tired. Shortly after that, we ended up homeless.

Tell me more about your experience being homeless.

Before I walk into this hell hole with you, let me say this… I ended up homeless not only as a child with my mom, sister, and brother but as an adult with my children as well.

The truck stop motel. We lived there for a little over a month. Our room didn't have a fridge; it was a rent-by-the hour motel. It was wintertime, *thank God*, because we used to pile up snow right outside our window and that's where we would keep our milk, cold cuts, and water cold. Our snowy windowsill was our fridge. I used to think it was so cool living at a motel. For some reason I thought it was a fancy thing, even though it was run down, smelled like trucks, and was really dirty.

The following experience is so ingrained in me that I remember it as if it were yesterday. My brother and I were alone at the motel. We had two beds in our room. He laid on one of the beds face down and said, "Hey, can you give me a massage? My back hurts." I innocently agreed. I sat next to him and massaged his back over his shirt. Although I didn't know what I was doing, I was trying my best.

He then said, "Sit on my butt instead and massage me from there." He lifted his shirt up and put it over his head then passed me the lotion bottle. I didn't even know how to massage someone. I had these tiny hands compared to his body.

Little did I know the devil was present.

After a few moments, he grabbed the white blanket that was sitting on the side of the bed. I got off him because I thought I was done and he felt better. But he turned over faced me and quickly put the blanket over his face. He said, "Go ahead, keep massaging me, but massage my stomach because it hurts." He grabbed my arms and gently placed my little innocent body on top of his erection, gripped my hips, and forced me to move in a way to please him. I didn't even know boys had different private parts then us girls at the time. I don't even recall knowing about private parts just yet.

It started hurting as he got more aggressive. I tried to get off him, but he just gripped my hips harder and forced me up and down. I can still hear him whisper, "Yeah, just like that."

I can still hear his deep breathing and thinking to myself how it hurt so much and so bad. I felt like I started to bleed. Tensing up, I tried a second time to get off. He said, "No, keep going; my stomach still hurts." I froze. I knew what he was doing was wrong; it hurt and felt terrible. I was so confused. The pain in between my thighs was unbearable.

What happened to my brother? He was supposed to protect

me like he did when mommy and stepdad fought. I had no idea what was going on, but it felt wrong. I was so scared I couldn't even cry. When he was done, he let me go and slowly got up off the bed and walked to the bathroom.

I went over to the other bed and laid there; I was huddled up in a ball under the blankets trying to hide. I felt my girls' parts throbbing in pain, and I didn't know what to do about it. He stayed in the bathroom so long I ended up falling asleep. He was the first one to violate me. He was not my biological brother. My mom took him in and raised him as if he were her son, *so to me*, he was my brother.

I was not too fond of this motel. It was no longer fun for me. This "massage" became a routine. Every time he laid on the bed and asked me for a massage, I felt sick to my stomach. I kept asking myself why—*Why does he do this to me?* I don't want to be there anymore. He was hurting me. I was just a child; I didn't even know what private parts were—what a devastating, heartbreaking month. That first time changed me. I was filled with guilt as if I did something willingly wrong. I felt like it was my fault.

I didn't know at the time but that was just the start of it.

Did you ever tell your mom or anyone what happened?

No, I never did as a child. But when I became an adult, I did. The reason why I didn't reveal it when I was a child to my mom was because of her response to a different painful memory.

One time when I was little, I told my mom that I hated going to my great-grandparents' house. She was curious as to why, but I didn't know how to tell her the truth, so I replied, "I get so bored there."

"You'll be okay; it won't be too long," she said, brushing me off.

She started to notice that I was getting upset. After some time, she asks, "Baby, what's wrong? Tell me."

"Mom, there is a reason why I don't like going there."

I was scared and afraid of the outcome because I wanted to tell her. I somehow built-up courage and spoke. "Mom, he touches me, and I don't like it."

She asked me if I was referring to the man my great-grandmother was married to. I shook my head, yes. She said, "Where?"

I put my hand gently on my groin as I looked down and said, "He always tries to put his fingers here."

Her response was unexpected. She laughed and said, "Oh baby, he plays around like that."

I lashed back, "He does it to some of us, and we don't

like it!" I got angry! How can she act like this was no big deal?

"Well, just push his hands away next time he does it." She replied.

We arrived at their home, and as soon as I walked in, he said to me in Spanish, "What do you have here? Let me see." As he went to reach for my vagina, I slapped his hand away and looked up at my mom.

My mom looked down at me and gave me a "calm-down" look. She didn't want to hear what I had to say before we arrived, and now, she just brushed me off. He did that in front of her and she did nothing about it! What she didn't know was he kept doing that to me inside my pants also.

My mom had the chance to do something about it, *but she didn't*. She didn't take me seriously. The pain I felt those times when he would stand next to me, reach down into my pants, and put his fingers in places they didn't belong was infuriating.

One time we were at a family gathering at their home. I remember I was wearing a skirt, and he put his hand in my skirt and asked me in Spanish, "What do you have there?" He moved my panties aside and put his fingers inside of me. I was trying to get him to stop. When he did, he looked at me with a smile and said, "Que rico" (which in English means, how delicious).

The only time I dared to say anything, I was utterly disregarded. I knew then that the only protector for me was me. I grew so much hate in my heart.

Were these the only times that happened?

No. My mom and I used to go to some guy's house. Let's call him the mystery man. I was left in his living room, always watching TV while my mom and the mystery man would disappear for a bit. Often, I would end up falling asleep on his couch. Two times I woke up to a man sitting on the sofa's edge. The first time I felt as if I was woken up. I looked at him, and he asked, "Want to watch something really quick?" I stayed quiet and turned to face the TV. He put on porn. I didn't know it to be porn at the time, but as a little kid, I didn't understand and looked at it with disgust.

The second time it happened, I asked him, "Do you know where my mom is?" I didn't know what was happening, why I was watching this, and more importantly, where my mom was. There are so many countless stories, abusers, situations, and horrid experiences I went through when it comes time to this category. I started growing more and more angry. I was being exposed to things children should not be exposed to. I didn't know how to handle these big emotions. I never said anything in fear of hurting my mom or worse... getting in trouble myself.

Out of all of your experiences, which one was the worst?

Out of all my experiences, including the one with my brother, the worst one was the one with the Woman. Simply because it was a woman. I thought only men would do these kinds of things to kids—*but a woman?*

My mom had a friend, and her daughters were around the same age as my sister and me. However, she had an older daughter as well. The older daughter was beautiful, with a cute little nose and a great laugh. Everyone loved her; she was one of those young ladies who turned heads everywhere she went.

She always got all the male attention. She was a charmer. "Come to the bathroom. My sister wants to show you something," the middle sister said to me. She grabbed a chair and put it in the bathroom. I then saw her sister utterly naked in the shower. She made sure I promised that I wasn't going to say anything to anyone. I was in elementary school at this point. She turned on the shower and began to show me her entire body. She opened her legs and told me to get a good look as she started touching her naked body all over and giggling as if she were shy.

I was just a child; and here I was, watching this grown woman do things to herself. I couldn't make sense of it. It was unbelievably uncomfortable to watch. I wanted to look away, but when I covered my eyes, the middle sister pushed my arms down and told me to watch as she laughed. I feared them because they were tough girls, so I did what I was told. I remember trying to make light of the situation by laughing and trying to cover my face. I thought to myself, this is freaking weird! Finally, it ended.

I love music. I loved to dance, sing and put on shows for people. Music was my escape; I loved the way it made me feel. It helped me disconnect from the world. Music helped me in all areas of my life. This season of my life I wanted to be a dancer.

I would beg my mom to let me be part of this dancing group. I used to dance with those two sisters in the city's Latino parades. Often, we would practice our dancing and learn new moves in the woman's house. Then one day we were in her house for practice and the vibe changed—we weren't dancing to bachata, merengue, or salsa. It was music that required twerking. I was told to put on a set of heels that were not your typical dancing heels; they were grown woman heels. She taught me how to dance in them. She taught me how to move my hips and touch the floor seductively while wearing these heels. I was left in that woman's house that night because my mom went out with her friends.

While I was in her house the woman told me, "Tonight, we are going to party, and we are going to show off all our dance moves and put on a show." She put lipstick on me and some eye shadow, gave me a pair of really short shorts, and then told me to take off my shirt. When I did, she giggled and said, "Girl, you don't even have boobies yet." I looked down at my bare chest and felt insecure. She went to her sister's dresser, grabbed a training bra. I remember looking at the bra and thinking to myself... *what the heck is this?* It was white and had a little bit of lace trim. She told me to put it on and focus on shaking my butt. I didn't even know how to put it on, but I figured it out.

The next thing I knew, I was called into the living room. The lights were off, and the room was filled with men and even boys a little older than me.

"Nobody touches her!" the older woman yelled out.

The music started, and I was encouraged to dance. I was so shy, scared and nervous about the entire thing. I slowly moved my hips and danced as I looked down at the floor. "Come on, do it like I showed you!" She yelled with a huge smile on her face. I started dancing the way she wanted me to. I was embarrassed and ashamed. She then came to me and whispered to take off my shirt and dance sexy. I did what I was told.

I stripped in front of grown men and boys of all ages. This ended up happening a few more times throughout the upcoming weeks. My innocence and love for dancing were now sexualized to please men.

As the shows progressed, so did the dances and techniques, and the touching started. I had grown men start to touch my thighs as I danced. I was so sad and started developing the persona of a stripper.

One of those nights, one of her guy friends got angry and said, "This is fucking wrong! Why are you having these little girls dance like this?"

She started giggling and replied, "No Papi, they like it! They have fun, right girls?"

I stayed quiet. He was angry and ended up leaving. Two

other guys, also upset at what they saw, got up and left with him. However, no one did anything to stop it, no one came to our rescue.

Before I could hit puberty, I had been so sexualized by my environment that I was numb to it all. I hated my life. I felt disgusting, ugly, dirty and unworthy… *I felt damaged.*

With all this abuse, when did you start to learn to fight for yourself?

I used to fear violence. Watching my mom and all her fights made me scared of men. I've seen how strong men are and what they can do, *especially to women.* That is not to say there aren't women in this world who are not abusive, and both have hurt me in diverse ways.

I developed a tough shell over time. I hated going to this one school. These two boys would pick on me badly. Every day after school, they would jump me. I remember being grateful for wintertime because I had more layers so the body shots wouldn't hurt too badly.

I hated those boys. I used to try my hardest to leave school as quickly as possible before they got to me. There was this section in the school playground where the fence was somewhat broken. I could squeeze past it by crawling on the ground and sliding my body under the fence. As soon as the school bell rang,

I would run out of school and try to slide under the fence before I got caught by a teacher. That was the only way I could get away from these guys.

But many, many times, I was not able to do that. I was forced to face those boys after school. I used to come home with bruises all over my arms, legs, and stomach. They rarely caught my face because I knew how to block my face. I told the teacher once because she saw bruises all over my arms. I told her what was happening, and she got emotional and hugged me. With tears in her eyes, she said, "Let's go to the principal's office together."

By this time point in my life, I had already been deeply abused and disregarded by my mom for telling her what my great-grandmother's husband did to me. I had no faith in adults. They used me, abused me, took advantage of me, and forced me to do things I didn't want to do. They hurt me. All of this was running through my little brain—*I was scared.*

The teacher held my hand as we waited for the principal. I could feel my palms getting sweaty, and I felt my entire body was shaking with fear. I wanted to tell her everything, but I didn't. I sat there in silence, comforted by my teacher as she held my hand. The principal finally arrived, and they had a conversation without me. Then, I was called into the office, where it was my turn to speak. I looked at him and said to myself, "I can't trust him." There was something about him I didn't like. He looked like a man who didn't care. I stayed quiet and only answered his questions. Nothing came out of that.

A few weeks later, I was asked to write something on the board in class. Afterward, the teacher pulled me aside and asked about the new bruises. I told her it was the two boys. She was furious. She took me by the hand, marched into the principal's office, and began yelling at him, telling him he needed to do something about it. She made me show him my arms and told me to lift my pant legs up, which revealed more bruises. I can remember the furious look in her eyes. I can't believe she was standing up for me. I saw her passion and her no-nonsense way of handling the situation. It was amazing for me to watch how someone could handle a situation without violence.

The boys finally got in trouble, but it worsened for me. At this point, my mom and all the adults were aware of the situation. My mom and my uncle started teaching me how to fight and stand up for myself. I started fighting back furiously. Yet no matter how much I fought, it didn't stop. The punches got harder, the kicks got worse, and I got stronger at handling my tears. *I was growing numb.*

My mom's coworker told me once in private, "Boys, no matter how much you fight back, it won't push them away." He then grabbed something out of his back pocket and handed me my first love, a pocketknife.

He showed me how to use it, and I felt empowered and fearless—*and yes,* I tried to use it! A group of girls tried to jump me in the school bathroom, and I took out my handy dandy pocketknife. *Yes,* I got caught. I felt powerful as I took that baby out to protect myself. I didn't care about the damage it was going to cause. I wanted it to stop! I wanted to be at peace. I hated going to school. I wanted them to be afraid of me, so they'd never mess with me again. Ultimately, the principal told me everything was my fault and that I wanted attention; that I was the problem.

At that moment, I chose to be a fighter. If I asked for help, they didn't believe me... if I fought and stood up for myself, I was the problem... forget it! I was tired of being scared. I was tired of being abused. I was tired of being alone. *I became a fighter.* I didn't care who it was—I fought them. The innocent version of me died long before anyway.

How bad did the fighting get?

I became a teenage mom and ended up in an abusive relationship. This one fight, this one moment, I thought I was going to die. I couldn't remember what we were arguing about or how it started. I knew it was getting heated and sent my daughters to their room. We moved our argument to our bedroom. He was getting in my face and yelling at me. I kept telling him to back away from me, but he kept trying to headbutt me.

The next thing I knew, he spit on my face—a fat loogie right on my cheek. Putting my hands on his chest, I pushed him away as hard as I could. He charged at me hard, then he began hitting me and pulling my hair. I tried to block him and push him away from me. I swung back... But he ended up grabbing me, lifting me up in the air like some crazy wrestling move, and slammed me on our bed. I tried everything I could. Kicking and screaming, I was trying to hit him back. Somehow though, through all of it, he finally got a hold of my neck and *squeezed*.

I couldn't breathe... I couldn't yell... I couldn't talk... I couldn't even fight anymore. I felt like my brain was going to pop. I felt my face getting really hot, and I tried to take his hands off my neck. Tears were falling down my face as I looked up at him. He said, "See what you are making me fucking do? See what you are making me do to you, you fucking bitch! I hate you!"

He was trying to kill me.

I thought it was going to be over for me. I thought I was going to die right there on our bed. I felt hopeless. With all the fighting I had learned throughout the years, I had nothing on this man and his ability to overpower me. He was obviously a better fighter. That same bed that we slept on... the same bed that he would *"love"* me on... was the same bed I felt like I was dying on. Then it happened, a tiny little scared voice yelled, "Don't hurt, my mommy!" I could see from the corner of my eyes; it was my oldest daughter.

Right away, he got off of me. And as soon as I could feel the release, I took the most enormous breath of my life. I was dizzy, trying to catch my breath. My heart was beating as if I was running from a wild animal. I rolled off the bed towards my daughter. I struggled to get the words out, but I finally I said, "It's okay, baby. Go to your room."

She ran away scared, her tiny little chinita eyes filled with fear. I can still see her beautiful tiny chubby face riddled with hurt. I thought to myself, *damn, she just experienced what I did at her age.* I laid there momentarily, caught my breath, and went to the kids' room. I walked into their room, and they were crying and hugging each other, *scared.* I hugged my babies and tried to show them I was okay. I found myself trying to be strong the way my mom tried to be strong for me. *Was I becoming my mom?*

My daughter saved me. I want to say it was the end of our relationship, but it wasn't. I ended up staying with him longer, and the relationship was hell.

Death

My amazing, loving, and strong grandma helped raise me alongside my mom, especially when my biological father didn't want to be in my life. She and my grandpa would take me almost every weekend and every summer. I love them both so much.

One day, while they were living in the projects, my grandma and I were doing our usual people-watching from the window. My grandmother had a pillow by the window, one for her and one for me. We would spend hours watching everyone in the neighborhood. She is that Latina grandma who knew what everyone was up to on the block, and it was hilarious. People watching is still one of my favorite things to do to this day. I love sitting in busy areas and just watching people. I enjoy observing how couples hold hands, kids act up in public, people speed walking by, arguments, or whatever else happens. I love watching humans being humans, just not in a creepy way.

My grandmother was the person who really taught me how to read people's body language. She was a master at it—*to me*. She taught me everything she knew about observing people. She would tell me what to look for when people were suspicious or how to tell if someone was up to no good. My grandmother also showed me how to tell if someone was happy or sad. She has always been a tough cookie too. She was and still is a fighter. As a stay-at-home mom for as long as I can remember, my grandmother taught me so much on how to take care of my home. I thank God every day that she is still here with us.

At the window, my grandmother and I saw my uncle, her son, hanging out with his friends. Of course, she was curious about what was going on. Out of nowhere, a car pulls up and starts shooting at them… it was a drive by. I saw one of the guys drop, and everyone ran. I can still hear the *pop pop pop* echoing from the gunshots. It wasn't my first time hearing guns going off; however, it was my first time seeing someone drop from a bullet. I couldn't believe my eyes.

After a few moments the friends gathered again over their boy's lifeless body screaming and crying. My uncle ran up to our apartment. I saw my grandmother yelling at him with tears in her eyes, begging him not to do anything about it. My uncle was crying, burning with anger and wanted to seek revenge at all costs. He was hurting, and my grandmother was scared for her son.

That was the first time I saw someone die in front of me. I was about five years old. I've witnessed many forms of people trying to hurt and kill others or themselves. Like this one time in middle school, a girl was slicing her wrists with a sharp piece of plastic. I looked at her and whispered, "What the fuck are you doing?" She didn't know what to do with herself after being caught. But I couldn't help but think to myself sadly… *me too girl, me too.*

One day, I was hanging out in a park in my hometown and saw the local gang beat the crap out of some guy all because he was where he shouldn't have been. You know how it is, one set versus the other. They beat him badly—*and took his boots.* His face was unrecognizable, and he was passed out in a puddle of blood. His clothes were ripped off his body. He looked dead. It looked like there were about 50 dudes that jumped him. Poor guy was lying flat on his back, barely breathing. Put it this way: as his body tried to breathe, only one side of his chest was moving up and down.

I got so emotional seeing what they did to him. He couldn't have been older than seventeen. I thought they killed him. It wasn't until years later that I found out he made it. He was in critical condition for a while, but he pushed through. It is unbelievable the amount of evil people can do. The way the guys laughed at the thought of them killing him. One of the guys grabbed my water bottle and splashed it on his Timbs, trying to wash the blood off. He grinned as he was stomping the guy's face in. *Pure evil.*

At this point in my life, I was attracted to gang bangers and thugs. One of the guys I was talking to at the time was a drug dealer. He wasn't handsome, but his swag was out of this world. We only went as far as talking. I attended night school to finish high school and earn my diploma. I had been thrown out of multiple schools for fighting, so this was my only option.

School would end at 9pm, and the drug dealer would walk me home. We would talk about his kids. He had a bunch and a whole lot of baby mommas. He told me how his one baby died from a shootout and how he wanted out of this life. His dream was to move to Pennsylvania, have a big house, a lot of land, and have all his kids living with him; although he was a drug dealer, he had a good heart.

He told me one time to close my eyes, and he snuck in a little tap kiss. When I opened my eyes, he expressed to me how grateful he was for our friendship, but that I wouldn't be seeing him for a while because he needed to handle some business. Turns out, he committed suicide; he couldn't find a way out of that life anymore... until he did. My heart was sad for him. Many friends took their lives and got their lives taken simply because they couldn't find a way out. Loss is so hard to deal with, especially when we grow to care and love these people.

What was the next season in your life like?

Growing up, my mom didn't have a lot of money. I had none. She was always working two to three jobs just to try to make ends meet. I started working young. I was cleaning houses, selling some weed occasionally, and when the time presented itself, I beat up girls for money. It didn't happen often, but it was a solid $20 when it did. I learned young that we needed to do whatever it took.

When I was a freshman in high school, I was old enough to get a decent job at McDonald's. I didn't mind the job; I just minded the damn manager that shoved me out of camera view so he could force himself on me; he was a creep. I was only sixteen, and he was in his late twenties. He grabbed my face and forced me to kiss him and was touching me all over. I was able to push him off and get him the hell away from me. I was so pissed off because I thought to myself, here we go again! These damn creepy guys trying to take advantage of me! It definitely took some fighting on my end but good thing I knew how to defend myself to a certain extent.

As a young adult, I became an EMT. I loved that job. It was a great career choice for someone like me that was numb to people. I've seen countless dead bodies and all kinds of pain. This one guy we picked up once stabbed me in the groin with my own pen! I knew he was off the moment I laid eyes on him. I saw evil within him.

This other patient we picked up was always so high. We

picked him up often. We caught him on a superhuman drug the day he attacked me. My partner at the time, whom I adored, manhandled the crap out of him. Then that guy ripped off his shirt and showed my partner a big Nazi sign tattooed on his chest. Yes, my partner at the time was a black man. I saw the pain in my partner's eyes when he saw that tattoo. He looked sad and disappointed. He didn't even look angry.

I was in shock seeing what happened. I couldn't even get mad; to me this was something you only see in the movies. I never met anyone in my life who was a white supremacist up until that point. I didn't even know what to do, and I think my partner didn't know either. My partner at the time was my best friend and that was the first time I saw his eyes filled with so much hurt. Where I grew up, "white people" were the minority.

This "Nazi patient" was the same guy who got so high on drugs he turned his penis into shredded beef. He was so high we had to stop him while he was having sex with stairs made of bricks. It was tough trying to apply pressure to his groin while he was trying to hump my hand; it was gross. Eventually that patient ended up going crazy, stabbing a bunch of people, and going back to jail.

We were on call for that one too. We picked him up. I asked him why he was doing what he was doing, and he replied, "I want to go home." That man had spent most of his life in prison. There was no life for him on the outside. He taught me a valuable lesson with that one liner. I understood for the first time that people only know what they know. I didn't feel bad for him anymore. He was comfortable being in prison and wanted to remain there for the rest of his life.

Was there a 911 call that has made a big impact on your life?

As EMTs, my partner and I were working a long shift. We got a call for an unresponsive infant. We rushed to the location, which was the projects, and ran up the stairs because the elevator took too long. Anyone who has been in the *'pjs'* knows it smells like pee and Fabuloso—especially if a lot of latinos live there.

And the rule is don't touch anything! Don't touch the walls unless it's with your shoes, and don't press the elevator buttons with your fingers; use your knuckles instead. We ran up those stairs trying not to touch the railings. I opened the door to go into the hallway, and a man was standing right in front of the elevator with what looked like a rolled-up blanket. He looked at me and said, "I don't know what is wrong with her," as he tossed me a baby as if she were a ball.

I unwrapped the blanket, and her little arm laid out lifeless. It was a beautiful baby girl, just a few months old, dead in my arms. Her face and lips were blue. She was swollen and had chinky eyes. I started doing compressions right away and ran down the stairs with her in my arms. We did CPR for what seemed like forever. The ambulance was filled with about five

EMTs, all trying their best to bring this baby back. Everyone was focused and trying to emotionally detach from the fact that she was basically a newborn baby. I've never wanted anyone to live as much as I wanted her to live. We ended up getting her stable enough to move her to the hospital.

Later on, we found out that her dad shook her to death. The same man that threw her at me in that hallway was the same man who gave his own daughter shaken baby syndrome. For the first time in a long time, I cried. *Here we go again*—my mind filled with thoughts about men and how hurtful they can be to women.

I later learned it's not the men or the women who hurt others, but the enemy within them. I loved that baby, even if my encounter with her was short. I hurt for that child. She ended up in critical condition, and we never got an update after that. I don't know if she made it or not. That first moment of her in my arms and seeing her lifeless body, blue lips and face is forever engrained in my memory. *Poor baby girl.*

Earlier you made a comment regarding the girl in your class cutting herself. Did you ever want to end your life?

At many points, I just wanted to end my life. I felt like I couldn't take it anymore. I didn't know what a good healthy relationship was, what safety felt like, or even if I was loved and valued. I kept everything to myself and just put my head down. I thought I wasn't meant to live a good life. My teenage years were when I started realizing that the things happening to me were not normal.

Before I became a teen mom, I wanted nothing more than to move forward in taking all the pain away. I often thought to myself, would anyone notice? I wanted to die too. I didn't know anything about death, but I knew I wanted it. Every time I closed my eyes and rested my mind, it was like flashback after flashback of all the evil working in my life. I felt like I was just constantly reliving my abuse and couldn't tell anyone about it. Even today, it's so hard for me to express my battles; I usually act like it's not a big deal. I'm older now and just realizing that the devil was so present in my life.

The first time I tried to kill myself, I swallowed an entire bottle of medication hoping it would do the trick. *It didn't.* So, the next attempt was swallowing 40 pills of extra strength acetaminophen. That didn't work either.

Then I realized I needed something a bit more extreme. I was just a kid and was talking myself out of hanging myself in the basement of our apartment building. I had many plans put in place and tested the waters many times. None were successful. I don't know, I guess if I really wanted to, I would have found a way. I didn't know how to manage any of the trauma and deep emotions. I just wanted a way out. I was so deep in a hole that I was already nonexistent and might as well have made it official.

All I know was that, honestly, I couldn't talk to my mom

because we already know what happened there. I couldn't say anything to my grandparents because I didn't want to hurt them. At this point, I knew the reaction would have been, "Why didn't you tell me?" The

> I am doing this interview because I hope my journey can help open someone's eyes to healing.

only reason I am even doing this interview is because I hope my journey can help open someone's eyes to healing. Staying in that harmful state of mind serves no purpose; it only destroys us more. I tried running away too, but all that did was make me feel guilty because I felt like I would hurt my mom even more, and to me, she didn't deserve that.

You mentioned you were a teen mom. How did your mom handle it?

Yes, as a teenager, I got pregnant with my first daughter. Even today, I still say that my daughter truly saved my life. I remember wanting someone to love me... someone I could love unconditionally... someone I could feel safe with... and who could feel safe with me. When I lost my virginity at 15 years old, I instantly got pregnant. I was scared but truly fine with it. I wanted her. I knew my mom was going to have me get an abortion. I did what I thought was best. I stayed physically active and nearly starved myself so my belly wouldn't show.

My mom started noticing when I was in my 2nd trimester. My belly was starting to pop. She grew suspicious because I started to get the pregnancy line down my belly. She took me to the doctor. They did blood work and told her I was indeed pregnant. I remember the day she confronted me about it. I was home and the house phone rang. When I picked it up, it was my mother. She was emotional and yelling at me saying, "When were you going to tell me?" I played stupid and acted like I didn't know what she was talking about. She then said, "I'm going to give you one more chance to tell me!"

I broke down, started crying and said, "I'm sorry mom." She and I were crying. She said we would talk about it when she got home. Man, I thought to myself, if I'm going to run away, it better be now. But I knew I wasn't going to make it with my baby. So, I stood there alone in the kitchen waiting for my mom to come home. When she finally did, it was so emotional for both of us. Endless conversations. Her emotions were raging. I can't blame her though; I was a kid. She told me I had to get an abortion.

"Mom, can I sleep with you?" I asked her the night before my scheduled abortion. I fell asleep on my mom's bed as she hugged my belly and cried herself to sleep. The next day, we went to the clinic and did my first sonogram. They looked at my mom and said they couldn't do the abortion; I was too far along. I was so happy! I felt such a relief. I did it! I lasted long enough so I couldn't get an abortion, I overcame everything. I was so excited to have someone who I could love unconditionally and someone who could love me too—*and we wouldn't hurt each other*. I was on cloud nine.

My mom cried herself to sleep for several nights. I hurt my mom with my decision. Maybe if she had understood how much I wanted to feel someone love me, she would have accepted it better. As a mom now to teenage kids, *man*... I can only imagine what was going through her mind at the time.

I remember hearing people saying negative things about me. I heard people trying to bring me down. I also listened to my mom fight for me. She had my back. She would tell people that I was a good kid and that I was going to be a great mom. I heard her tell people that I wouldn't need anyone, that I could not only take care of myself but of a baby too. Although my mom was sad sometimes, she believed that I was going to be a great mom. That meant a lot to me. She had my back even though what I did was not ideal.

After I had my baby, I started to hustle, go to school, and work. I cleaned up my actions and became a good girl. I graduated with my high school diploma and walked across that stage with my pregnant belly... # 2.

I know what you're thinking... *Life got harder really fast for me.* I did everything in my power to protect and provide for my babies. People would shake their heads at me and say things like, "Babies, raising babies." The old me told them to fuck off because I was doing what I needed to do to provide. My mom helped me so much. I worked two to three jobs at a time just to provide. My mom would watch the kids for me sometimes as I went to work. Besides the occasional hanging out with my cousins, I never went out and partied or did anything stupid after that. I just went to work, came home, and took care of my babies. My mom loved my kids and really enjoyed being a grandmother.

Being a mom of two kids by the time you graduated high school must have been a tough experience?

Yes, my pregnancy with my second daughter was tough. When I was pregnant with her, I went in for a follow-up Ob-Gyn appointment and I had a feeling this one was going to be different. They called my name and escorted me to the doctor's office instead of an examination room. The doctor was inside, and she greeted me. She mentioned the nurse would be right in to join us. Sitting and staring at the doctor, waiting for her to say something as she was reading my file, I became anxious. Then, the nurse walked in and broke the awkward silence. She sat down, and then the doctor said with her heavy Latina accent, "Mama, I don't know how to say this to you because you are so young and pregnant, but I'm going to be blunt, okay?"

I said, "Yes, of course."

"You have cancer," she stated.

She started to explain in more detail, but I stopped listening after hearing those three words. It took me a while to come back to the conversation mentally. She said, "We can't do any treatments because you are currently pregnant, but..."

Before she could say anything else, I aggressively said, "I'm not killing my baby! I want my baby to live." I felt a huge knot in my throat, and I knew I would rather die myself than to abort my baby. Even though my 2nd pregnancy was not planned, I would never do anything to hurt my babies, in the womb or out of the womb. They are mine to protect.

She shook her head, replying yes to my response. She mentioned because of my decision there wasn't anything that could be done until after I give birth. She made it clear that I was high risk and could possibly lose my life. I didn't care, my babies are my babies, and I had no problem dying so they could live.

After that appointment, I walked home. There I was alone again crying my ass off caressing my belly as if my baby could feel it. It was as if I was comforting her. I remember telling my belly how much I love her and how I would always protect her. I told myself I'm not strong enough; I'm only 18 years old, I need someone. I wanted someone to talk to so bad, but I knew I had only me and my babies. My thoughts went to God.

Up until this point you really hadn't leaned on God at all. What was your conversation like with Him in this situation?

I was pissed off!

I yelled, "God, how dare You?! How dare You try to take my babies away from me! How could You let this happen to me? What the hell did I do so badly that You want to take me away from my kids? I thought You were supposed to love us. How dare You?! Fix this! I will not die and leave my babies. So, You fix it!" I was beyond angry; I was ready to go toe-to-toe with God. I was demanding He resolve this problem.

Safe to say, I was infuriated; I had enough! My life had been challenging enough, but I was still a teenager. I was too young to die, even though I felt like I had died long before that. I thought to myself I finally have something to live for. My babies are my everything; nothing matters more than my babies. They gave me a purpose to live.

My entire pregnancy, I was terrified. I remember telling my mom to please take care of my babies if anything happens to me. I would cry myself to sleep holding my daughter while she hugged my belly thinking I may not be here to see them grow up. I was so scared. I looked up in the air every day and rolled my eyes at God. I was so mad at Him. I blamed Him and I wanted Him to step in.

Do you know what it's like thinking that you may be dead soon after giving birth? I thought about all the things I would miss out on in their lives: their sporting events, graduations, first kisses or boyfriends, the first time they get their heart broken, their weddings, and the first time they accomplish something big. I thought about what kind of women they would grow up to be without me. Would they be protected? I didn't want to die anymore! I wanted to live, I wanted to be a mom. I finally found my purpose, and I felt like God had threatened me. I was so scared. Everything I ever wanted was in those two babies of mine, and they were about to lose me.

I don't know if it was my demanding faith, but by the time I gave birth to my second daughter, they couldn't find a trace of cancer. Shocked was an understatement. I was confused; *what happened? Where did it go?*

I didn't know it to be God's doing then; I was still angry and confused about where I stood with God. So, I just said it must be something related to science and kept moving. It came back two more times after that. A few years ago, I got a partial hysterectomy.

You were in an abusive relationship. Why did you stay?

Here is the truth about my mentality at that time, I was a completely different person in a different situation. How am I even alive? With all the issues going on, I wanted my children to be raised with a dad, so I chose some shitty relationships. I settled.

He beat me. *It was okay*; having a man in the home was more important than how I felt. He was verbally abusive, manipulative and narcissistic. It was okay. I would make it work because having a dad at home was more important. I was so used to being abused that I played the comparison game with my relationships, comparing bad-to-bad and sugarcoating everything, all because I desperately wanted my babies to have a dad. I was trying to protect my babies from feeling the emptiness of not having a dad around. I was willing to sleep with the devil and act like it was better than not having him around.

I was so used to men abusing me that I always said to myself, "As long as he doesn't touch my babies, then we are okay." What a heartbreaking mindset. Clearly, I didn't love myself. I just settled knowing those men weren't good for me and were going to hurt me. I tried so hard to protect my babies, but unfortunately, I couldn't completely.

What happened to your kids that you felt like you couldn't protect them completely?

I always did private checkups with my kids. I would talk to them and ask them if anyone ever touched them or if anyone was mistreating them. I told them some of my experiences, so they felt comfortable talking to me. I assured them that whatever it was, they could trust me.

I had these constant dreams that something was wrong. At this point in my life, I now had three babies. One day, my babies were laying on my oldest daughter's bed, hanging out at night. I walked in and laid down next to them. With all three of my babies cuddled up, I said, "Okay, guys, time for checkups!"

I proceeded to ask my questions, and they all said no... except this time my oldest daughter stayed quiet. We all looked at her, and she said, "Oh no, nothing." She tried to giggle it off, but we could tell she was lying. My middle daughter looked at her with such concern and looked at me telling me with her eyes something was wrong. I kicked everyone out of the room. Then she started to burst into tears as I was holding her and trying to keep my cool. She told me that she was touched.

My heart dropped, and I asked, "By who?" It felt like forever before she finally answered me. She said the name of my mom's new husband. My mom had finally settled down and gotten married to what I thought was an okay man at the time. She had been with him for many years. I asked my daughter for as much detail as possible. She gave me every heartbreaking detail. I told her to relive that moment, go back in time, and tell me exactly everything. She painfully did.

I trusted him; how could he hurt my baby like this? You can't imagine the rage I felt at that moment. The worst part was that he did it while my mom was in the kitchen. It was under the same roof while she was there. The anger I felt was something I couldn't put into words. We tried to manage the situation the right way and get the authorities involved. They couldn't do anything about it because it was her word against his and there was no evidence. My daughter was hoping to get justice, but she didn't. We told my mom, hoping she would leave him, but she never did. They are still together today.

This man tried to break her—*my baby*—but he didn't win! My oldest daughter, *may God continue to bless her,* taught me such a valuable life lesson during this battle we fought. She was much stronger than I was for sure!

You can just imagine what I wanted to do to the person who hurt my baby. The self-control I needed to have was something out of this world. But we got through it.

What about your other children?

Darkness was upon my second daughter; I could see it in my baby girl's eyes. I would constantly pray over her and all my babies. One evening, I felt God tell me go to her. I got up out of my bed and went to her room and laid down next to her, hugging her, just being present with her.

The next day, I was in my room doing some work, and she came to me and said, "Mom, I need to show you something." She pulled down her pants and showed me all the slashes that she had made on her thighs. She admitted to me that she has been cutting herself and going through depression. She assured me no one had ever abused her. She said she didn't know why she was doing what she was doing; she just felt like cutting herself.

The night before, her thoughts got out of control and that's when I entered her room and laid down with her. That simple action led her to the decision that she needed to tell me before it got worse.

My heart sank for my baby girl. I was angry... I was sad... I felt like I had failed as a parent.

I thought to myself what would I have done if I found my princess gone one day? I wouldn't have been able to live with myself. The heartache a parent feels when their child is suffering with depression is something to be only described as 'heavy.' I went through an internal struggle, questioning if I had done something wrong or maybe I could have done something different. Was I not a good enough mother? I was completely blaming myself for her feeling the way she did. I was thinking maybe I didn't communicate enough… Maybe I didn't provide a good enough life… I felt like this was all my fault. I was assured by a counselor that I have been a great mom, and that depression sometimes just happens. But still, I couldn't help but keep thinking maybe I could have just been better.

Both my girls have leaned on Jesus and have been in counseling ever since these events occurred. As a family, we came together to help both my girls get through the attacks of the enemy.

You said, 'Darkness was upon my second daughter; you could see it in my baby girl's eyes.' What do you mean by that?

I'm not sure if I want to discuss this part.

Why is that?

Because I would sound like a nut job to you and maybe some of your readers.

Maybe. But it would be worth it if it could help someone, right?

Agreed. There may be people who can relate. My commitment to start this interview was to be completely honest, no matter the cost. So here it goes. I see spirits. Most people would ask, "What, like in the movie 'The Sixth Sense'?" Yes and no. Let's start from the beginning, shall we?

Ever since I can remember, I have been able to see spirits. It wasn't until my adult years that I encountered a good spirit. Other than that, they have all been demons or demons pretending to be something else that they are not.

One time, I woke up in the middle of the night. I was about eight years old. At the time, my bedroom was by the kitchen. I opened the door because I thought I heard a noise. I saw a light coming from my living room on the other side of the apartment. I slowly walked to the living room. It caught my attention precisely because it looked like something was floating. It wasn't objects, more like dark cloudy circles.

Someone sat on the couch when I finally got to the living room. He was dressed in all black with a black hoodie. I didn't go up to him; he came to me. His face was inches from mine. It was a pale face with dark eyes; they looked black. He had a very sharp jawline. The first thought in my mind when I saw him was, 'Wow... he is beautiful.' He just stared at me, tilting his head back and forth. It was a tense, deep-eye connection. The more I stared, the more scared I got. His face slowly morphed like a reptile, with small horns hiding under his skin above his forehead. I knew he was beautifully evil.

I was constantly getting attacked by spirits. They would come at me in my dreams. When I would open up and share my experiences with people, some believed me and some didn't. For that reason, I stopped telling people about this "*gift*" of mine. However, those who did believe me tried to guide me. I now know they were guiding me towards witchcraft.

I had a demon attack at 14 years old in the apartment I lived in. I was genuinely being tormented there. That apartment brought out suicidal thoughts in me. Once, I was lying on the bottom bunk in my room when my cat came in and jumped on my chest, hissing. I was on the phone with my then boyfriend, and he asked what was happening. I told him my cat was hissing, and it freaked me out. I was scared as I was petting my cat telling her she's a good girl, hoping that would calm her down. My cat was staring at something above my head. Something must have spooked her because she got scared and ran out of my room. I got up, closed the door, and laid back on my bed. Then, suddenly, I felt like something was choking me.

A couple of days before that incident, I was telling my

grandfather, my mother's father, that I kept seeing evil spirits and thought our apartment was haunted. He gave me a necklace with a picture of Jesus and put it on me.

I couldn't breathe while lying on my bed. Suddenly, I heard what sounded like a bear growl. Then, I felt like something was sitting on my chest, and I felt like I was being strangled. I kept feeling a burning sensation in my upper chest. I couldn't say anything... I couldn't scream... I couldn't do anything... it was as if I was paralyzed. But in my mind, I was screaming loudly. It was as if my soul was on fire and being ripped out of my body.

Suddenly, my mom burst through my door and started screaming. Her entire body filled with goosebumps as she saw me getting physically attacked by a demon. As soon as she opened the door, it released me. After we both calmed down, I had scratch marks on my neck and upper chest, and bruises were starting to form. The experience was quite unsettling. My mother took me seriously moving forward when I told her that our apartment was haunted.

My mother had a few older Spanish church ladies visit our home to "cleanse" it. One of the women passed out and spoke in an unfamiliar language with a changed voice. My house was filled with demons. I was being visited by many spirits—which was intriguing my curiosity. You would think that I would be so terrified and want nothing to do with any of it. Instead, it piqued my interest... so I tried to communicate with them. I used a Ouija board to dive deeper into the paranormal, leading to unexplainable visions and knowledge about people that I shouldn't have had known. I believed more in the devil than I believed in God.

I saw it was getting out of hand and started ignoring these spirits. Then I realized that I had become a target to those who were into witchcraft. I had a bunch of people constantly approaching me. When I got older, I started working at a bar/restaurant. One of the bartenders approached me and handed me $100. I asked what it was for. She pointed at an older gentleman sitting across the bar and said, "It's from him." I walked over to him and immediately noticed something strange in his eyes. I could see the demon in his eyes.

I thanked him for the money and told him he didn't need to do that, as I wasn't his server. He then started to tell me that he was a "*Babalawo*" and that he could see that I had a gift. I joked and asked him, "Oh, yeah? What gift is that?"

He said, "You have the gift of spiritual vision; you can see things that no one else can."

Right away, my heart sank. I got goosebumps all over my body. I thought to myself, how the hell did he know that? I felt as if the secret that I had been keeping my whole life had just been exposed… like a teenage girl who wrote everything in her journal only for someone to find it and read it to the entire world. *Exposed.*

He continued telling me how I could become an influential leader in his world and that I should embrace it instead of running away from my gift. He wrote his number down on a napkin and then handed it to me, promising he could train me and show me how to be powerful while using my gift. I have to say, I was freaked out.

My mom took me to a few *"witches"* growing up because of my visions. They all tried to recruit me, as they could see my gift and promised I could be powerful. However, I knew it was all the works of the devil. I can easily see evil. It all seemed very tempting—*especially since I felt like God was punishing me*—but something always held me back. Something felt wrong about it, but most importantly, my gift revealed the truth. I could see the intentions behind every single one of them. They tried hiding from me, but I could still see and feel them. I thought if this was truly a gift, where are the angels? Why couldn't I see angels? Why was I only seeing the bad ones?

Any final thoughts before I move onto the questions of how you healed?

I have been through a lot in my life, and there are many stories that I could share. These experiences have shaped me into the person I am today. I only cared about my children and that they were my safe space. They help me to become a better version of myself every single day.

However, I began to dislike people so much that I started to hate being around those I did not care about. I didn't trust anyone and kept everyone at a distance. Some people knew about my experiences, but this was the first time I went into this much detail. I was always scared that no one would believe me or would disregard my trauma.

Most people thought I was cold and had a tough exterior. If someone were too good to me, I would push them away. I believed I was not worthy of goodness even though I wanted it. I was never vulnerable, and I didn't trust nor like anyone. Even in relationships, it was very hard for me to be intimate with someone on a sexual level because often I would check out mentally. During sex with someone I cared about or loved, I would have this overwhelming guilt that I was enjoying myself and my brain would just go on "*autopilot*." It was as if I wasn't even there in those moments. Afterwards, I would cry myself to sleep. I didn't know why at the time.

Most people tell me that I am hard to read until they get to know me. I could see this to be true because I got very good at hiding my emotions. I kept my feelings to myself and put my head down and did what needed to be done. I didn't like myself and felt that I wasn't a good person deep down. I would walk around and act like everything was okay. I tried to put on a smile and show people that I was doing great! *But I knew the truth.* There have been many people who have hurt me or didn't have any concern over my wellbeing because they said, "She is strong, she can handle it."

I was strong because I had no choice. I was cold and heartless because I couldn't be anything else. I was disconnected because I couldn't connect with anyone. They hurt me. I became who I was because I had no choice.

I got into fights and hurt people in different ways. I was okay with it. I shrugged my shoulders and acted like I didn't give a damn. I've said things I shouldn't have said... I treated people harshly... and although as I got older, I tried to get better... I couldn't erase the mistakes that were made to me and to others. There may have been some people that I let my guard down with, but even then, I pushed them away. What can I say, "Hurt people hurt people."

I am deeply sorry to everyone I have hurt and mistreated in my life. I can't fix the past, but I promise I try every day to be better and bring value to other people's lives.

BORN AGAIN

Let's talk about your healing journey. How did it start?

There was a simple introduction that changed my life completely. It opened my eyes and forced me to start my walk. I didn't know it was coming but, *when it did*, I knew I needed to move forward. In the beginning, it sucked.

I was at a company event in Arizona. As I was walking in the lobby with my business mentor at the time enjoying the occasion, we were greeting everyone we knew. It was a great time. Suddenly, we saw a man I greatly admired. My mentor took me straight to him and introduced us. As he shook my hand, I was nervous. I noticed how tall he was, and it was like he was a gentle giant. I said, "Hi Papa, I'm Andrea." Everyone called him 'Papa.' After some small talk, he asked me about my religious background, and asked me if I believed in Jesus. I jokingly replied, "Do you mean, does Jesus believe in me because I've been through some things!"

Papa then turned to my business mentor at the time and said in a serious yet soft tone, "I would like to speak to her alone. Can you make sure no one disrupts us, just for a few minutes." Then Papa looked around the lobby and saw two chairs in a corner and grabbed my hand and walked me to those chairs. I thought I was in trouble, but I felt such a comfort in him holding my hand. It was as if a father was holding the hand of his daughter.

We sat down and I could tell he was getting his thoughts together. He asked me a couple of questions about my beliefs, to which I answered that I was a "good Catholic." I went to church only for funerals and weddings. I chuckled because I knew I was being sarcastic. I'm sure he picked it up also.

I realized he could tell a lot from my previous response. I honestly felt like an idiot. I thought maybe I offended him. I took a moment and looked him in his eyes, and I could see such love, gentleness, and kindness. I didn't know it at the time but now I know it was the Holy Spirit I saw in him. Staring into his eyes brought me an uneasy feeling of peace, something I wasn't familiar with. After a few silent moments, he then told me that the pain I endured was not God punishing me, but the work of the enemy and that God loves me and has a plan for me.

This revelation moved me to tears, which was unusual for me. *How did he know?* How did Papa know I was dead inside? How did he know I suffered? I was in an uncomfortable vulnerable position. I didn't tell him anything more than what I just told you! I felt that he could see all my pain that I was trying to hide. I didn't tell him about anything that happened to me growing up, how could he have known? It baffled my mind, and I began to shake.

He then reassured me about God's love and asked if I wanted to accept Jesus into my life, to which I humbly said yes. His embrace afterward felt like he was hugging my soul, and it was the best hug I have ever received. Everything I had buried all those years surfaced. It felt like the best hug I have ever gotten in my life. In his arms I felt safety... I felt security... It was as if he was hugging my broken soul and putting my broken pieces back together again little by little. I can't begin to tell you the love I felt in that embrace. It was as if GOD himself was hugging me. I couldn't keep myself together. I went to my hotel room and just sat there in my puddle of tears. I couldn't make sense of what just happened to me. All I know is that I couldn't stop sobbing. In my room alone, I said, "Okay, God, who are you?"

At that moment, I decided that I was going to find out. I then went on a journey to find out who Jesus is. Papa told me I needed to go through the Son if I wanted to know the Father. I didn't know what that meant, but I was forced to face my demons. Once I finally got home, I opened my Bible and didn't know what I was reading. It felt like a foreign language. So, I bought an entirely new Bible, the NIV one with red lettering.

In Genesis chapter 1, it talks about the creation of the Earth. God created the sun, the night, the land, the sea, the animals, and everything. Then He created us. God created us in His image. It also said he blessed us. He gave us the gift of His creation, authority over it all, and the ability to be fruitful. In Genesis 1:31 it says, "God saw all that He had made, and it was very good. And there was evening and morning—the sixth day." That took me to an entirely new place mentally.

Wait… wait… wait… God saw all He made to be good? So, it made me ask the question, "Am I good?" God created me too. So all this time, I thought God didn't want me. I thought I was a punching bag. I thought I was worthless. I thought I was a mistake. I thought I was being used as the devil's playground. Do you mean to tell me my Creator thinks I am good?

God created the entire world and said the world needed

me, too. I questioned it: *God, are you sure? Do you know what I've done? Don't you know what has been done to me? How could I be good?* I looked at myself as garbage for so long.

If you feel this way, pay attention to what molded you to be you.

When you were born, you were born perfect and without sin. Our experiences in life molded us to be the products of our environment. I am telling you that you have something great inside of you; God's amazing spirit lives within you. Stop thinking you are unworthy. God created heaven and Earth. Guess what? He created you, too. We may make mistakes, but God does not. You are beautifully and wonderfully made. So, if you are sitting there battling with your self-worth, remember God created all your beauty, and He still looks at you and says you are worthy. God created the entire world and said, "You are good."

God sent His son Jesus to die on the cross for our sins. Most people don't understand this, so let me explain...

The Old Testament in the Bible is all the shadow of Jesus. It is giving us lessons and preparing us for the coming of Christ. Why did Jesus's sacrifice need to happen? Because humans became separated from God. For us imperfect beings to have a direct relationship with God, we needed an intercessor. We needed someone to be the middleman for us so we may have direct access to God. But we are sinners—*constantly sinning*—and God is a god of perfection and righteousness. So, He sent His son Jesus who was perfect and without sin. He was sacrificed for the sins of the world, and because of that, we are forgiven and can come to the Lord boldly.

God created us. He loves us so much that He made sure we could have a relationship with Him. If He didn't, then why would He sacrifice His son for us? Why would His son die a cruel and torturous death? Jesus was flogged, beaten, and spit on; His flesh was ripped and torn. Yet even as He was nailed to the cross, He still said, "Forgive them, for they know not what they do."

WHAT?! People tortured him… *killed him!* Jesus could have stood up for himself. He was innocent, he did nothing wrong! Jesus could have said, "ENOUGH! You people don't get it! Why should I die for you?! Why should I sacrifice myself for you ungrateful, unloyal, sinful people! You don't deserve this!" *But he didn't.* He didn't say any of that. He willingly died for us.

It made me think… who would I be willing to die for without question? My kids. I would die for my kids without even thinking about it. They are my life, my loves, my everything. Is that how God feels about us? *About me?* We are His creation. He loves us. Jesus died for us. He died for me; I AM LOVED.

His love for us is so phenomenal that we are now blessed with the Holy Spirit within us. Yes, that's right—the Holy Spirit of God is within us!

Understand this: that person in your life, past or present, who told you that you are less than others—*is a liar.* Please don't believe him or her. You may have made mistakes and did things you shouldn't have or are not proud of. I get it. I was right there with you. However, as soon as I understood that my mistakes did not define who I was in the eyes of God, I forgave myself. Letting it go took me a minute, but I realized I was loved. I am so loved. My father on Earth may have left me, but my Father in heaven never did. Some people may dislike me, but my God loves me.

You must grow to know it to be true about you, too. You are so preciously created. There will never be another one like you. You are unique.

If you are struggling with anything we have covered so far, stop reading this and take some time to take one big look at yourself. But don't look at yourself with your own eyes and your judgment. Look at yourself from the eyes of God, the One who created you in His image; the One who created all creations and said it was good... *including you.* Look at yourself from His eyes. Picture Him hugging you, wiping away your tears, and telling you, "I created you good! Very good."

Are you ready to accept Jesus into your life?

THEN SAY THIS PRAYER OUT LOUD:

Heavenly Father, I am a sinner. Please forgive my sins and cleanse me from any unrighteousness. Come into my heart now, Lord. I believe that Jesus is Your son, who died on the cross for my sins. I believe He rose again, and Your Holy Spirit lives within me. Be the Lord of my life. I will serve You, obey You, and follow Your Word from this day forward. I pray all this in Your mighty Son's name, Jesus Christ. Amen.

SURRENDER PRAYER

Dear heavenly Father, I have not taken care of myself as you wanted me to. Until now, I may not have considered myself of value, but I know now that You created me of value and goodness. Thank You for loving me so much. My heart is open now, Lord, and I lay myself at your feet. If I battle to see my value moving forward, please remind me that You deeply love me through Your Word. I surrender myself to You. Let me love those around me—*including myself*—so Your love shows through my actions and Your Holy Spirit. In Jesus' name, Amen.

If God is so good, why do bad things happen?

That was one of the biggest questions in my journey with Jesus. I am no Bible scholar, nor have I ever attended any Christian schools, so my response to this is strictly my findings in the Bible and my experience.

There is good—God—and there is evil—Satan. I won't sugarcoat it; there is evil in this world. It is shown in the Bible many times. For example, in Matthew 4:1-11, the evil one visits Jesus during His fast and tries to get Him to break His fast by eating. The evil one tries to get Jesus to throw Himself off the highest point of the temple. And then, finally, the devil tries to tempt Him with worldly values such as kingdoms and splendor to get Jesus to worship him instead of God. The crazy part is that the evil one tried to use scripture and the word of God to tempt Jesus.

In Matthew 8:28-34, two demon-possessed men confronted Jesus, and Jesus rebuked them.

There are so many examples of evil outside of the Bible. I'm sure you have encountered evil. As you have read in the first part of this book, so have I.

God gave us free will. He gave us the gift of making our own choices. So, if someone has evil in their hearts, they are more likely to do evil things. You will do good things if you have goodness in your heart. Either way, that is the truth. You may not like that because most people can't accept that people have the freedom to do some messed up stuff. At one point or another, we come to points in our lives where we make decisions.

Decisions to be good or decisions to be crappy and allow evil to rule over us. God gives us the choice either to choose Him or not. We are not the Sims game, and this isn't a game of God wanting to control us. He wants us to choose. He loves us enough to give us the right to choose.

This is a challenging pill to swallow. God does not promise that there will be no evil or that we won't encounter hardships—quite the opposite. The Bible is full of instances where God tells us how to overcome Satan and his wicked ways.

Do you think any of your abuse was brought on by your own doing?

I used to think I brought it on to myself. How could I have thought that? I was just a child. As I got older, I should have been able to identify some evil, though. However, going through traumatic experiences can mess with your way of thinking and belief system. I was young and abused, but no one saw the signs they should have. I was left alone with demons repeatedly as a child; it was not my fault. I was hurt, scared, and didn't know any better.

Looking back now I can say neither did my mom or anyone else who was supposed to protect me. I felt as if I had no one to turn to. As I got older, hearing all the horrible things my cousins went through and my aunts being sexually abused, it scared me even more. What a demonic generational curse!

Learning that made me even more emotionally disconnected. I am not angry at my mom or any other adult around me who was supposed to take care of me. I do not blame any of them. What I don't agree with is the manipulation of the word forgiveness.

My abuse warped my mind and made me believe that I was the problem. After so many instances of abuse, I became numb to it. By the time the next abuser came along, I just laid there and let that person do whatever they wanted to me until they were satisfied. I had programmed my mind to disconnect during those times so well that it felt like an out-of-body experience. I would pick a spot on the ceiling that I would stare at, or I would imagine in my mind something else. I would go through my to-do list or what I wanted to do the rest of the day.

When those who abused me mentally were abusing me physically, I had to learn to "*act*" like I was enjoying it. The more I acted like I liked it, the faster it would be over with. It wasn't until after it was all done that I would come back to myself and cry myself to sleep.

The demons tried to break me, and they almost won. I blamed myself for so long. I found myself taking full responsibility as if I were the abuser. I hated myself; I felt dirty. Inside, I felt disgusting and broken, but outside, I acted like everything was okay. I knew how to play pretend. I knew how to satisfy others and do what they wanted me to do even though I was dying inside. To me I did not matter, because in my mind, I never did.

I was battling two versions of myself: one crying out for someone to love me and wanting to feel safe and secure; and the other side of me, cold-hearted and disconnected, soulless and seeking revenge.

As a Christian, I now understand that evil had full authority in my life since birth. I didn't have a prayer warrior who could fight for me then. I learned that Jeremiah 1:5 states, "Before I formed you in the womb I knew you; before you were born, I sanctified you; and I ordained you a prophet to the nations." Evil knows our greatness and tries to break us as children, so we turn away from our Creator. It tries to plant seeds of doubt, fear, worry, pain, and suffering within us so that we stay in the presence of the enemy instead of the presence of our heavenly Father. Being stuck in these emotions is all part of the devil's plan, not God's. The devil tried to get to me even before I was born because he knew the enormous potential inside of me.

"For I know my plans for you," declares the Lord, "plans to prosper you and not to harm you, plans to give you hope and a future."

Jeremiah 29:11

Now, don't get me wrong. I've committed many sins, and they were 100% my fault. I took responsibility for those. However, it was clear that the evil one wanted to stop me, so I had to let go of all the pain. I had to try to heal my brokenness. I had to try to feel again and not be numb and punch out. I had to face those demons—and myself.

What do you mean you took full responsibility for your sins?

Once I processed it fully and saw myself in the eyes of God and how valuable I am, I had an 'aha' moment. I realized how much I messed up. It wasn't good. Suddenly, I could remember every horrible thing I had ever done. I felt so embarrassed, and the shame and guilt were sometimes unbearable. I spent an entire week wrapped up in a cloud of emotions.

One of the things I've done is make amends. I made a few phone calls and apologized to some people, including those whose phone numbers I didn't have. I went on social media and ensured my apologies were from the heart. To my surprise, every single person forgave me.

There were some things I had done that no one knew about, and boy were those the hardest ones for me. Because it was only God and me, I had to ask God for forgiveness for things I knew were unforgivable in my eyes. That was one of the most challenging weeks of my life.

We are so hard on ourselves sometimes. We make mistakes, and we think our mistakes are who we are. They are not.

Repeatedly Jesus says, "Your sins are forgiven."

Not only does He say it to us, but He also wants us to know we must forgive everyone who sins against us. Yes, that one is a bit harder to swallow though.

When a group of men brought a paralyzed man to Jesus, He saw their faith and said, "Take heart; your sins are forgiven."

Matthew 9:1-8

If we confess our sins, He is faithful and just and will forgive us our sins and purify us from all unrighteousness.

1 John 1:9

We have a forgiving God. He loves us. He knows we will mess up but forgives our sins. If your past is holding you back from building a relationship with Jesus, then you address it. Take the time to open your Bible and search for scriptures stating that you have been forgiven. You can't change your past; you can't undo everything that was already done. However, you can take ownership of it. Confess to God your sins and know that you have been forgiven.

If we want to accept Jesus into our lives, we must get to know Him. Since Jesus is forgiving, and we are trying to be like Jesus, we must also be forgiving. Who better to start with than ourselves?

How can you forgive those who hurt you?

Our Father in Heaven. Hallowed be your name, your kingdom come, your will be done, on Earth as it is in heaven. Give us today our daily bread and forgive us our debts as we also have forgiven our debtors, and lead us not into temptation, but deliver us from the Evil one.

Matthew 6:9-13

The key lines here are "Forgive us our debts as we also have forgiven our debtors." If we know that God forgives us, we must also forgive. I know what you're thinking: how could I forgive that person? Look what they did! Look how they hurt me. Trust me, I know how you feel. I've daydreamed about what I could do to get my revenge back on those who hurt me. But I hurt God also, and He still forgave me.

Then Peter came to Jesus and asked, "Lord, how many times shall I forgive my brother or sister who sins against me? Up to seven times?" Jesus answered, "I tell you, not seven times, but seventy-seven times."

Matthew 18:21-22

For if you forgive other people when they sin against you, your heavenly father will also forgive you. But if you do not forgive others their sins, your father will not forgive your sins.

Matthew 6:14-15

This is a tricky subject but stick with me here a bit longer. There is a reason why Jesus is saying that we must forgive. The reason is that Ephesians 4:21-32 says: "Let all bitterness and wrath and anger and clamor and slander be put away from you with all malice, and be kind to one another, tenderhearted, forgiving one another, as 'God in Christ forgave you.'"

Is bitterness of God? What about wrath, slander, and anger? No, right? None of these are of God. So, if they are not of God, then who are they of? You guessed it right.

The evil you are holding on to is holding you back from building a genuine relationship with God. Remember, the enemy's job is also to try to distract you. So, if he can get you to lose focus on Jesus and focus on the hurt, the pain, and the anger, then he is winning! You are letting him win. You can't be impure in the loving presence of God and receive and give forgiveness if there is hate in your heart.

Some things are hard to forgive and understand. But if we don't forgive, what is the alternative? How can we move on? Don't get me wrong, forgiveness does not mean reconciliation. I am not in contact with my abusers, but I forgave them... but boy, was it hard. I looked at myself and thought, God forgave me. In the eyes of God, sins are sins. So, I took that step in forgiving. Trust me, it wasn't easy. Sometimes I needed to remind myself I forgave that person already because flashing back in time, *like my brain likes to do sometimes,* still hurts.

Here is where most people get confused... The manipulation some people use with forgiveness is that if you forgive them, it means you should invite them over for Sunday dinners and bring your abusers around your children. However, you can forgive then remove yourself. If someone tells you otherwise, you must ask yourself is this person allowing evil to use them against you? If yes, it's better to forgive and part ways.

Matthew 18:15-19 tells us clearly how to manage a situation with those who hurt us. I would suggest opening your Bible and reading it for yourselves because I will paraphrase it here broken down into steps:

1. Talk to the person alone.

2. If they don't listen, bring one or two others with you to speak to that person again.

3. If that still doesn't work, get your mutual community involved. If the person still refuses, then you treat them as someone who needs to be kept away.

You can forgive people even if they are unwilling to ask for it. You do not have to hurt yourself by being around people just because they hold a specific title in your life or because they have some form of authority. It is perfectly okay to forgive and move on.

My mom chose to stay with her husband even after he hurt my daughter. This was a challenging situation, but I had to make the tough decision to remove them from our lives. Forgiving my mom for not believing my daughter was hard. Forgiving the abuser, *who denied the abuse*, was even more complex. However, my daughter's reaction to the situation showed me what being a Christian means.

She forgave him. Watching her forgiveness gave me the strength to do the same. Seeing my daughter forgive him and my mother for not believing her opened my eyes. It's much easier to forgive when someone sins against you. But when someone sins against your loved ones, it takes an entirely new strength… much like that of Christ. I want to thank my daughter for teaching me this lesson not just through her words but through her actions and strength. *Life tried to break you, baby, but it did not win.*

Why would forgiveness be mentioned in the Bible if forgiveness wasn't necessary? One way that helps me forgive others is reminding myself that the person doing the hurting may not be aware of the spirit upon them. Everything happens in the spirit realm before the physical realm. That's why Jesus says to pray for our enemies. Why would He say that? They need their demons rebuked, and Jesus knew that. Pray for enemies to come to Christ, then you'll see a renewed person—the actual person God created them to be—not the one they became because of the enemy's influence.

You mentioned your brain goes back in time with your trauma, what is that like?

I imagine talking to my younger self. One of the things I always felt I needed was someone to protect me and rescue me from everything that happened. Growing up, I wished I had someone I could feel safe with. This confused my mind about what I thought a protector was. I thought a fighter meant a protector. I thought a man with a short temper or someone who doesn't take crap from anyone was a protector. Boy, was I wrong! This led me to relationships with men I had no business being in as I started getting older.

I constantly searched for the one partner with whom I could feel safe. Unfortunately, I was choosing the wrong kind of tough guy. I was unconsciously trying to find someone to protect that little girl in me. Someone who could go back in time and help heal my brokenness. But what I was asking for was for my past to be healed so I could be *"fixed."*

Papa once told me, "God daughter, the Bible is the best self-development book you'll ever need. When you read the New Testament, picture yourself with Jesus, watching Him heal the sick, cast out demons, and teach. Picture yourself in His presence as if you were there with them." This helped me get closer to Jesus.

I asked myself what if I'm able to do that with myself and my past? What if I could go back in time—*in my mind*—to that little broken girl and be the person I needed to be for myself… to say what I needed to hear after each incident? So, I decided to try it, and boy, was it a walk-through hell.

I closed my eyes and returned to that truck stop hotel where my brother wasn't my brother. I can't change the past but can influence my subconscious mind to heal. In my mind, I was standing in the corner of the motel room and watching it all happen again. I pictured myself standing tall, the adult version of me in that room with the little version of me and him. I watched it all happen again. It was painful; the adult version of me cried. But this time, I was in control.

When everything was done, I imagined my brother going to the bathroom. My adult self sat down next to my younger self on the same bed where it all happened. The adult me hugged the little me and said, "Talk to me."

The little me asked, "Why did he do that?"

The adult me replied, "Because he's broken, baby."

The little me asked, "Did I do something wrong?"

In tears, I replied, "No, baby, you did nothing wrong."

I proceeded to tell the little me precisely what I needed to hear. "Baby, you may not know what just happened. I know you're in pain both physically and emotionally, but I'm going to be honest with you. Worse things are going to start to come your way. None of it will be your fault. There will be people you love and trust who will hurt you. But I want you to know that none of it is your fault. Some things are outside of your control. You are going to go through more pain and life is going to get hard for a little bit, but I want you to know that you are so loved. I love you.

The things that are coming your way are going to feel like they can break you, but you won't break. God has a plan for you. You're going to grow up and be a great mom of beautiful babies… you are going to be successful… and most importantly, you are going to find the Greatest Love. You will finally have a Father who loves you, protects you, and dies for you. Don't let these moments eat you up. You're going to be okay, baby. I promise."

In my mind, after saying all of that, I just sat there and hugged little me and let her cry it out until she was okay. I used this technique with every traumatic event in my life. I even went back in my mind and revisited the sins I committed. Still, after watching it all unfold again, I mentored myself and brought myself before the Lord. I pictured myself kneeling at the Lord's feet, confessing my sin, crying out, and my heavenly Father telling me my sins are forgiven. I pictured Him listening to me and comforting me.

This technique I used was challenging because as much as I wanted to do things differently and be the superhero who showed up and rescued me, it didn't change what happened. So, I allowed myself to walk through my hell. But this time I came to myself, hugged myself, and told myself it would all be okay. I pictured the young version of myself crying, yelling, screaming, venting, whatever I needed to do, while the big version of me was listening and having compassion for myself. I mentor myself and use what I have learned through Christ Jesus to help comfort me. In those instances, at the end of every scenario, I hugged myself and cried until it was okay. I pictured God with us in that hug, completely consuming us with his light, warmth, and love.

All I needed after all of it was done was just someone I could talk to, someone who could hold me and have empathy for that hurt little girl. Someone who would tell me that I am loved and will be okay and how a beautiful life awaits me on the other side of all these emotions. I didn't have it, but through this technique, I was able to be that for myself. Our subconscious mind is so powerful. It doesn't know what is real and what is not, it goes based on what is fed. I chose to feed it with positivity and love. It was painful, but it worked. Jesus healed me deep inside and showed me God has love for us. It truly, truly helped heal me from my past.

Spending time with Jesus, I intentionally healed myself from the inside out. I was always willing to do anything to feel God's love, even if it inconvenienced me. I worked on being more wise, compassionate, strong, loving, and having a higher self-worth and identity. The only one I knew who could help me in all those areas and more was Jesus. Even though I felt like I didn't have the time to commit how I wanted to, I put myself in check and called myself out. I didn't want to just meet with God on Sundays. I was swamped throughout the day and focused on finding a solution. I knew my life wasn't going to change unless I did first. My mind needed to change, my heart needed to be turned from stone to flesh, and my heart needed to be filled with love.

Matthew 15:17-19 talks about how what comes out of the mouth comes from the heart and defiles us, so I knew that if I wanted to be better, I needed to change my heart.

Matthew 14:13, Mark 1:35, Mark 6:45-46, Mark 14:32-34, and many more scriptures in the Bible talk about Jesus going to be alone with God. He intentionally went off and spent time with God daily. I wanted to share that personal experience with God. I decided to follow Jesus' example of spending time alone and praying. I made the choice to wake up every morning at 5 am to spend time with God intentionally, and it has profoundly changed my life.

This journey helped me accept things I cannot change and even led me to pray for my enemies, wishing for their repentance and release from their demons. I realized that I harbored anger and revenge toward people, so I prayed for help to see others through God's eyes and to change my perspective. Then guess what? A lot started to happen. I began to see people differently. I have prayed this prayer daily for over a year. I started falling in love with people.

I began to see their value; I started to see their beauty. I started to see them from a spiritual sense. It became easier for me to be compassionate for people, it became easier for me to be more understanding, and oh boy, did I grow a passion for trying to see things from all perspectives. I became slow to make decisions and faster to pray. I learned that evil works hard, and I noticed he works through people.

I started becoming gentler, kind, and forgiving. Especially with myself. Jesus forgives me daily, and I should be able to as well. I can't change the past. I can't change the things I've said, the people I've hurt, or the damage I've done. I can only be apologetic, ask you for forgiveness, forgive me, and move on. I'm sure someone is reading this right now, whom I've hurt. I'm sorry. I didn't know any better. I do now. I promised myself I would never hurt someone else intentionally ever again. I am not perfect, and neither are you. No matter what we do, we can never be perfect, but we can try to be our best. l know I will make mistakes, just like you will too. But Jesus says you are forgiven; move on and try your best not to do it again.

I still get angry sometimes, I have a potty mouth, and I must remind myself of who I am daily. It's an ongoing battle to keep the enemy away, but I know that Jesus is in my mind and in my heart. WWJD - Those cute bracelets that people wear is fantastic. They serve as an excellent reminder to keep us in check. But how would you know what Jesus would or would not do if you didn't know Him? If you want perfect, undeniable, miraculous healing, don't lean on people; lean on Jesus. I am a firm believer that our faith needs friends, but I also know that every single Christian I have ever met in my entire life is human. Humans don't always get it right, but Jesus uses them—*us*—many times and guides us through the Holy Spirit. How do you do this?

I didn't just read the Bible as a story; I would read a story in the Bible and then ask myself the following questions.

1. What do I learn about God?

2. What do I learn about people?

3. What do I learn about relating to God?

4. What do I learn about relating to others?

5. What does God want me to understand?

6. What does God want me to believe?

7. What does God want me to desire?

8. What does God want me to do?

9. Is there an example to follow?

10. Is there a sin to avoid?

11. Why do you think God or Jesus is doing or saying that?

If you want to change what's happening inside of you and make it better, then consistently put in the work every day, and most importantly, have grace towards yourself. Love yourself, but don't be self-consumed. Appreciate yourself, but don't idolize yourself. Put God first above everything you do. Don't just say it; do it. Look for the answers to your questions. Let Jesus be your coach; let the Holy Spirit guide you in the Bible and life.

"Whatever you ask in my name, and I will do it for you" - Jesus Christ.

How did you start to rebuild this new self-identity?

Now that Jesus has become my coach, I saw somethings in me that I didn't like. I had a voice in my mind telling me things that I ended up believing and it became my self-identity. All this trauma and everything I had gone through really messed up my self-image, my self-love, and what I thought my value was. That was crap. One of the things I needed to do was to identify my strengths. I knew I was strong, when adversity hit, I pushed through, put my head down, and was forced through it. However, inside, after it was all said and done, I felt like all I was doing was crying silently, feeling weak and alone. When I would pray, I would sit there and tell God all my problems.

Jesus said, "Truly I tell you, if you have faith as small as a mustard seed, you can say to this mountain, 'Move from here to there,' and it will move. Nothing will be impossible for you."

My mountains were my problems. I stopped telling God how big my issues are and started telling my problems how big my God is.

With the help of prayer, my conversations are more like this, "God, I know this problem I'm having is nothing but the evil one trying to get to me. I know, Lord, you have already won this battle for me. Thank you, Jesus, for being the ultimate defeater. Evil, get away from me! I already won. You do not influence me. I rebuke you, devil, in the name of Jesus.

Lord, I know I'm not where I am supposed to be right now, but I know you are guiding me, and I am following. The devil has no authority in my life. I am a child of God. Satan cannot touch me!"

Lord, my child is facing challenges, and the enemy is trying to pull my child away from you. But I know you love my child more than I can possibly love them. I know you are with them. I know your Holy Spirit is guiding, protecting, and helping them during this time. I rebuke the evil one and place my child at your feet. Thank you for always being with them. In Jesus' name, amen."

You have to claim victory over your problems. When Jesus was rebuking those demons, he spoke with authority. Jesus came to die for our sins, but He also came to show us how to have authority over the enemy. He didn't ask, he demanded. It would be best if you demanded those demons leave you and your family. They will try to get in your head and try to get you to spiral out of control emotionally, but you need to recognize it and say, "Not today, Satan. You can't control me; you can't influence me."

After a while, you'll notice that when the enemy tries and fails to get to you, he will try to get to you through the people around you. You have to recognize that and rebuke the enemy from all those around you. The Holy Spirit is mighty and powerful, and as long as you allow the Holy Spirit to use you, everything that Jesus did here in the flesh, you can do too. Take a moment and pray those demons away from you. Those in your mind and those from your past, break those chains and claim they no longer have authority in your life. Know that you are a child of God, and they will no longer have a home within you. In Jesus' name, amen.

Affirmations

In this book, I will give you the greatest gift my Godfather ever gave me: Biblical Affirmations. Say these to yourself daily with authority and picture them as a reality. Let your spirit, mind, and body feel and believe it.

+ I am complete in Him, who is the head of all principality and powers (Colossians 2:10).

+ I am alive with Christ (Ephesians 2:5).

+ I am free from the law of sin and death (Romans 8:2).

+ I am far from oppression, and fear does not come anywhere near me (Isaiah 54:14).

+ I am born of God, and the evil one does not touch me (1 John 5:18).

+ I am perfect, holy, and without blame before Him in love (Ephesians 1:4; 1 Peter 1:16).

+ I have the mind of Christ (1 Corinthians 2:16; Philippians 2:5).

+ I have the peace of God that passes all understanding (Philippians 4:7).

+ I have the Greater One living in me; greater is He Who is in me than he who is in the world (1 John 4:4).

- I have received the gift of righteousness (not reward) and reign as a king in life by Jesus Christ (Romans 5:17).

- I have received the spirit of wisdom and revelation in the knowledge of Jesus, the eyes of my understanding being enlightened (Ephesians 1:17-18).

- I have received the power of the Holy Spirit to lay hands on the sick and see them recover, cast out demons, and speak with new tongues. I have control over all the power of the enemy, and nothing shall by any means harm me (Mark 16:17-18; Luke 10:17-19).

- I have put off the old man and have put on the new man, which is renewed in the knowledge after the image of Him Who created me (Colossians 3:9-10).

- I have given, and it is given to me; good measure, pressed down, shaken together, and running over, men give into my bosom (Luke 6:38).

- I have no lack, for my God supplies all of my needs according to His riches in glory by Christ Jesus (Philippians 4:19).

- I can quench all the fiery darts of the wicked one with my shield of faith (Ephesians 6:16).

- I can do all things through Christ Jesus (Philippians 4:13).

- I show forth the praises of God, who has called me out of darkness into His marvelous light (1 Peter 2:9).

- I am God's child, for I am born again of the incorruptible seed of the Word of God, which lives and abides forever (1 Peter 1:23).

- I am God's workmanship, created in Christ unto good works (Ephesians 2:10).

- I am a new creature in Christ (2 Corinthians 5:17).

- I am a spirit being alive to God (Romans 6:11; Thessalonians 5:23).

- I am a believer, and the light of the Gospel shines in my mind (2 Corinthians 4:4).

- I am a doer of the word and blessed in my actions (James 1:22, 25).

- I am a joint heir with Christ (Romans 8:17).

- I am more than a conqueror through Him Who loves me (Romans 8:37).

- I am overcomer by the blood of the Lamb and the word of my testimony (Revelation 12:11).

- I am a partaker of His divine nature (2 Peter 1:3-4).

- I am an ambassador for Christ (2 Corinthians 5:20).

- I am part of a chosen generation, a royal priesthood, a holy nation, a purchased people (1 Peter 2:9).

- I am the righteousness of God in Jesus Christ (2 Corinthians 5:21).

- I am the temple of the Holy Spirit; I am not my own (1 Corinthians 6:19).

- I am the head and not the tail; I am above only and not beneath (Deuteronomy 28:13).

- I am the light of the world (Matthew 5:14).

- I am His elect, full of mercy, kindness, humility, and long-suffering (Romans 8:33; Colossians 3:12).

- I am forgiven of all my sins and washed in the Blood (Ephesians 1:7).

- I am delivered from the power of darkness and translated into God's kingdom (Colossians 1:13).

- I am redeemed from the curse of sin, sickness, and poverty (Deuteronomy 28:15-68; Galatians 3:13).

- I am firmly rooted, built up, established in my faith, and overflowing with gratitude (Colossians 2:7).

- I am called by God to be the voice of His praise (Psalm 66:8; 2 Timothy 1:9).

- I am healed by the stripes of Jesus (Isaiah 53:5; 1 Peter 2:24).

- I am raised with Christ and seated in heavenly places (Ephesians 2:6; Colossians 2:12).

- God greatly loves me (Romans 1:7; Ephesians 2:4; Colossians 3:12; 1 Thessalonians 1:4).

- I am strengthened with all might according to His glorious power (Colossians 1:11).

- I am submitted to God, and the devil flees from me because I resist him in the name of Jesus (James 4:7).

- I press on toward winning the prize to which God in Christ Jesus calls us upward (Philippians 3:14).

- For God has not given us a spirit of fear; but of power, love, and a sound mind (2 Timothy 1:7). It is not I who live, but Christ lives in me (Galatians 2:20)

What are your final thoughts?

My favorite Bible verse is this passage is from Matthew 14:22-36:

Immediately Jesus made the disciples get into the boat and go ahead of Him to the other side, while He dismissed the crowd. After He had dismissed them, He went up to a mountainside by Himself to pray. Later that night, He was there alone, and the boat was already a considerable distance from land, buffeted by the waves because the wind was against it. Before dawn, Jesus went to them, walking on the lake. When the disciples saw Him walking on the lake, they were terrified. "It's a ghost," they said and cried out in fear.

But Jesus immediately said to them, "Take courage, it is I. Don't be afraid." "Lord if it's you," Peter replied, "tell me to come to you on the water." "Come," He said. So, Peter got down out of the boat, walked on the water, and came toward Jesus. But when he saw the wind, he was afraid and beginning to sink. He cried out, "Lord, save me!"

Immediately, Jesus reached out His hand and caught him. "You of little faith," He said, "why did you doubt?" And when they climbed into the boat, the wind died down. Then, those in the boat worshiped Him, saying, "Truly You are the Son of God."

When they had crossed over, they landed at Gennesaret. When the men of that place recognized Jesus, they sent word to the surrounding country. People brought all their sick to Him and begged Him to let the sick touch the edge of His cloak, and all who touched it were healed.

If you feel this healing journey is too hard, remember that Peter walked on water. Everyone on that boat was scared, and Simon Peter boldly had the mindset of let me go to Jesus. He did what we would call the impossible. *You can, too.*

Things in your life may be scary right now or make you feel as if you have no control. But just like Peter, if you want to run to Jesus, you must have faith that He will have your back. Peter was walking on water. It wasn't until he shifted his focus to the storm around him that he began to sink.

Stop focusing on the storm around you and keep your eyes focused on the goal, healing, and Jesus. There will be fierce winds and rain, and it will feel like you may not make it out of your situation. Still, I am telling you, as a woman who has been mind-screwed my entire life, I know now more than ever that my eyes must stay the course.

"You of little faith, why do you doubt?"

Man, that hits me hard. I don't want to doubt; I don't want the storms around me to keep me in the boat. I want to walk on water; I want to be with Jesus. I don't want the storms in my life to confine me to a boat and leave me scared and lonely. I've been there already, and I know you have too. I know you understand the feeling of being surrounded by storms and not knowing how to get off the boat.

The Bible does not say that someone told Peter to ask Jesus, "If it's you, tell me to come out onto the water." He did that on his own. He saw everyone afraid, so he stepped up and said, *"Let's go!"* Because of his boldness, his protective nature, and being a person who was in control, he took the biggest leap of faith.

Peter, the rock... the outspoken leader of the disciples... the one who was known to challenge Jesus and question Him... the one who chopped off a guy's ear for trying to arrest Jesus... yes, that Peter. The same Peter who denied Jesus three times when Jesus was captured and beaten.

Jesus told Peter he would deny Him three times before the rooster crows. Peter denied it as predicted in Matthew 26: 69-75. After Peter denied Jesus by yelling at the crowd and telling them off, the rooster crowd and Peter remembered what Jesus said.

Peter left and wept bitterly. Can you imagine the guilt he felt with that mistake he made? Could you imagine after all this time with Jesus, Peter denied Jesus at the time He would have needed him the most? While Jesus was being spat on, beaten, and treated like crap by a massive mob of people, Peter denied Him.

Peter loved Jesus; he even cut off a guy's ear for Jesus. Peter was like Jesus' right-hand man, and he denied Him! The fear Peter must have felt—the guilt, the shame. I bet it was unbearable. I bet you feel like your actions have been hard, too.

Look, everyone makes mistakes. Everyone has been through a battle—some battles harder than others—but that doesn't mean one is greater than the next. What makes it feel like that is your perception.

Spoiler alert: Jesus dies and is raised from the dead three days later.

Jesus and Peter had time to talk. Jesus asked Simon Peter, "Simon, son of John, do you love me more than these?"

Peter said, "Yes, Lord; you know that I love you."

Jesus said, "Feed my lambs."

Again, Jesus said, "Simon, son of John, do you love me?"

Peter said, "Yes, Lord; you know that I love you."

Jesus said, "Take care of my sheep." He said to him a third time, "Simon, son of John, do you love me?"

Peter was hurt because Jesus asked him the third time, "Do you love me?"

He said, "Lord, you know everything; you know that I love you."

Jesus said, "Feed my sheep. Very truly, I tell you, when you were younger, you dressed yourself and went where you wanted. But when you grow old, you will stretch out your hands, and someone else will dress you and take you where you do not wish to go."

Jesus said this to indicate the kind of death by which Peter would glorify God. After this, Jesus said to him, "Follow me."

Peter was struggling with the guilt of denying Jesus before He died. Then, Jesus allowed him to redeem himself. Peter denied Jesus three times, but Jesus allowed him to express his love for Him three times.

What a beautiful God we serve. Jesus welcomed Peter with open arms and allowed him to express his love for Him. God knows you've made mistakes; He knows people. *He created us.* He knows us better than we know ourselves. He saw what was in Peter's heart, just as He sees what's in yours. He sees your greatness, love, kindness, and faults and still loves you. You don't have to endure pain, guilt, suffering, or doubt. Jesus got you.

As I mentioned at the beginning of this book, I am not in a position to give medical advice on healing from trauma. I want to share with you that when all the counseling, conversations, and anxiety medication weren't working anymore, I chose Jesus. The more I immersed myself in the New Testament, the more I healed. You don't have to carry this burden anymore. You are completely free now. Give the baggage to God; let Him take care of it for you. Let Him be the healer, as He is the best at it.

I chose to forgive all those around me and to accept that Jesus forgives me too. I made a choice when the pain was unbearable, and I couldn't take it anymore. I became completely numb to everything around me, and that was enough. You can't live life like this and enjoy it. You don't know to truly love until you have experienced the love of Jesus. I am not a Bible thumper; I am just a woman who had an exceptionally long walk-through hell and felt like that's where I belonged.

The devil is a liar.

You do not need to be afraid anymore. I am telling you right now that you are the only person holding you back from living the life you always wanted. You may need to take some action steps to move forward, but at the end of the day, you are just one decision away from making your life the greatest it has ever been. Do not be afraid; you no longer have to hold on to this. You can let it go. I got so tired of trying to control everything all the time; it was time for me to give up my control to the only One I knew who could do this life better than me, and that is Jesus Christ.

I give myself to Him.